In an Angry Season

CAMINO DEL SOL

A Latina and Latino Literary Series

In an Angry Season

Lisa D. Chávez

THE UNIVERSITY OF ARIZONA PRESS

Tucson

First Printing
The University of Arizona Press
© 2001 Lisa D. Chávez
All rights reserved
∞ This book is printed on acid-free, archival-quality paper.
Manufactured in the United States of America
06 05 04 03 02 01   6 5 4 3 2 1

Library of Congress Cataloging-in-Publication Data
Chávez, Lisa D.
In an angry season / Lisa D. Chávez.
p. cm. — (Camino del sol)
ISBN 0-8165-2152-2 (acid-free paper)
1. Hispanic Americans—Poetry.   2. Women—Poetry.
I. Title.   II. Series
PS3553.H3463 I5 2001
811'.6—dc21   2001000485

British Library Cataloguing-in-Publication Data
A catalogue record for this book is available from the British Library.

The epigraph on page vii was excerpted with permission of Scribner,
a Division of Simon & Schuster, from *Solar Storms* by Linda Hogan.
Copyright © 1995 by Linda Hogan.

Publication of this book was made possible in part by a grant from
the National Endowment for the Arts.

FOR STEVE

Some of us would . . . be fed only bitterness from
the dark bowl of history.
                                —Linda Hogan, *Solar Storms*

Contents

ACKNOWLEDGMENTS xi

I CAPTIVITY

The Crow's Bride 3
A White Pony 7
The Strange Daughter 11
In the Antelope Hills 13

II AT THE WORLD'S FAIRS

In the Mammoth Temples of the Columbian Exposition 19
The Conjuror of the New Century 22
Photo of Inuit Woman and Child at the
    Midwinter Exposition, 1894 25
Cannibals 28
Geronimo at the World's Fair 31

III SURRENDER

Surrender 37
She Pictures Herself with Him 40

Reunion at the Girls' Boarding School 42

In the Season of Suicides 45

Lost Country 48

Helen in Captivity 50

The Century Plant 53

The Tattoo Artist 55

The Bad Wife 57

The Good Wife 59

Tsunami 61

Psalm 63

IV THE NEW WORLD

The Alchemist's Assistant 67

The Witch's Lament 69

In Your Absence 71

Young Wife Dreaming 73

Over the Chilkoot Trail 76

The White Professor Holds Forth on Indians 79

White Lies 81

Seal Woman Accepts the Sacrifice 84

In an Angry Season 89

Acknowledgments

Some of these poems have appeared in the following journals and collections: "The Crow's Bride," *¡Floricanto Sí!: A Collection of Latina Poetry;* "Geronimo at the World's Fair" and "The Tattoo Artist," *Blue Mesa Review;* "In an Angry Season," *The Americas Review* 24, nos. 1 & 2 (Copyright © 1997 *The Americas Review,* reprinted by permission of Arte Público Press), reprinted in *The Floating Borderlands: Twenty-five Years of U.S. Hispanic Literature;* "Cannibals" and "The Alchemist's Assistant," *Luna;* "Over the Chilkoot Trail," *Prairie Schooner;* "Surrender" and "The White Professor Holds Forth on Indians," *Clackamas Literary Review;* "White Lies," *Colorado Review.*

The poems in the first part of this book were the result of much research on captivity narratives and the World's Fairs. I would like to thank the University of Rochester for support for graduate study, during which time I did the research that led to these poems, and Albion College for start-up funds, which allowed me to travel to Chicago for further research on the 1893 World's Fair.

Some of the details included in "The Crow's Bride" were drawn from the book *White Captives: Gender and Ethnicity on the American*

Frontier by June Namias (1995). I also found Robert Rydell's 1984 book, *All the World's a Fair: Visions of Empire at American International Expositions, 1876–1916,* instrumental in my thinking about the World's Fairs. Actual details were taken from *A History of the World's Columbian Exposition,* Rossiter Johnson, ed. (1897), which includes a catalog of exhibits at the 1893 Fair.

I

Captivity

The Crow's Bride

I have written a true statement of my captivity; what I suffered and what I was spared from suffering, by a Friendly or Christian Indian ... I trust that the world will not censure me for speaking kindly of those who saved me from death and dishonor. . . .
  —Sarah F. Wakefield, *Six Weeks in the Sioux Tepees, 1863*

I dreamed of the crow, sooty ravisher
of gardens, scavenger, but in dreams tame,
familiar, a kindred soul. Chaska.
His name, like harsh cry of crow.

Waking, my face wet with tears. Why
must I remember, again and
again, why these tears, bitter
as the blood—so much—that watered
the earth that summer. So long ago,
my captivity. Chaska. Of him and me
so many evil things were said:
that I wished him spared
because I loved him. I could not
love a savage, though I could respect one.
The day the massacre began, who was there
to save me? Who heard the war whoops,
Hapa's drunken laugh as he pointed
his gun, my neighbor Gleason's body slumping
into mine, his chest a bloody bowl.
The rifles swivel towards me.
Chaska's intervention. Who but me saw,
smelled, the burning farms, the broken
bodies, a feast for flies. All this

he saved me from. And why? A remembered kindness
from me, the doctor's wife.

My own people were so long—oh, so long!—
in coming. Where were they as I huddled
in the heat and stench of Chaska's tepee
of ill-cured hides, my babes curled around me.
I did not love him. Could not, him a savage: fierce
bird gaze, dusky skin, hair long
and dark as a winter's night. His caresses
I would have borne, nonetheless, if my babes
be saved. But he did not caress. Morning
after morning, I woke to the sun, steaming
us awake, the drone of flies, his unblinking
gaze. Only once, did he touch me,
the night Hapa reached for me, eyes mad
with whiskey. Chaska rose, his shadow
covering me like a blanket. "I will take her
for myself." Hapa demanded proof.
Even the smoke froze, suspended in the air.
Then gently as the leaf falls, he slid between
me and my babes, laid at my side. Fire
whispered, the children's sleeping moans
stilled, Chaska's breath spiced sage
near my face. His hand on my hip. Satisfied
Hapa departed, and Chaska slipped away
to his bed across the fire. Beside me
the earth turned sweet.

So when the tribunal said Chaska should
hang for the murder Hapa committed, is it any wonder
I screamed those words? "Captain Grant, if you hang
that man, I will shoot you." In my passion

for justice, I said that, though my words
fluttered uselessly away, like my reputation, lost
in the storm of accusations: Indian lover,
adulterer, whore. All that I bore.

They hanged him by accident,
so they said, his pardon forgotten. And my habit
of tears began. An Indian wife would have painted
her face with ash, tore her hair, her clothes.
I did not. When I received news
of Chaska's death, my husband,
Dr. Wakefield, was drunk. Seeing my tears,
he beat me, left my face stained
with bruise. Tears proof of my guilt.
Whore. Such was my life
before my captivity. And after.

Chaska they hung because of me,
that I dared defend him guilt enough.
The last time I saw him, chained, he asked
why I had forsaken him, reminded me
how he'd sold his coat for flour
to feed me, how he'd saved my life.
I could not save him, though I tried.
Even his poor body, I could not
save, dug up a year later by white men
who took his scalp. You can see it,
at the historical society, his fine
crow-colored hair fading
before the curious stares. As for me,
you see how it is. An old woman, reviled
by my own kind. My husband dead, a suicide.
My children scattered. Myself, memory ridden.

[handwritten annotation:] You can't undo whites hanging blacks, whipping them on their backs fucking them on their backs, but you can ...

Over the hanging ground, a Dakota woman tells me,
thirty-eight eagles circle, souls of the dead.
Eagles. I wonder. For again and again, I dream
of the crow, so familiar, so dear.
I did not love him. Across the fire's ashes,
in the dark of those hot and terrible
nights, he did not touch me. And yet
I dream of him still. Chaska. I am twice
widowed. Mourning, in black I dress.
The crow's bride.

A White Pony

*If the old-time Sioux Indians possessed any noble traits . . . I utterly
failed to discover them, after residing among them for years.*
    —HELEN M. TARBLE, from *The Story of My Capture and Escape
    During the Indian Massacre of 1862*

That winter hunger was my lover,
caressing my hips till they jutted
like blades. My husband gone trading
and me alone, hungry for food, for talk
and touch. I stood on the hill
near the Sioux camp, watching.
I was afraid of their dark faces,
their alien speech—harsh as a handful
of stones shaken in a pan.
But my stomach clenched like a fist
at the smell of cooking meat.
An old woman—face furrowed
as worm-eaten wood—approached,
pulled at my arm. Made a movement
of hand to mouth, pointed to the village below.

Hunger led me there; loneliness kept me.
I even stayed some nights, rolled in a buffalo skin
next to the smoking fire. I called them dirty,
savage, yet daily they melted snow
to bathe, fed me from their small store of meat.
Naturally I dropped into their ways.
By summer I spoke their tongue.
Old Woman's husband taught me the way
of the healing plants. Granddaughter, he called me.

Harder each time to leave them—
my husband's face growing barbaric
with beard, our language strange
and sharp. Fifteen I was, and easily led astray.

When babies came, keeping me home, still
I kept their ways. In white moccasins,
wrapped in a blanket like a squaw,
I drowsed before my fireplace,
animal spirits drifting in the smoke
of kinnikinnick rising from my pipe.
I dreamed in Dakota, syllables sliding
on my tongue like tender pieces of meat.
The women came to my kitchen, gossiped.
The names they spoke—so outlandish—
Brass Tinkling, Pretty Shield, even
Muskrat Liver! Lightning Blanket.
Of him much was said. A warrior.
Haughty. Keen featured. Less ugly
than the others, I thought.

Summer, 1862. So hot the earth cracked
and dried like an uncured hide.
Corn withered in the fields. The blood
the earth drank. So thirsty, it asked
for more. Neighbors slaughtered
before my eyes. By my treacherous Indian
friends! I was taken to the camp, captive.

In Dakota, I cursed them,
but the young men only laughed.
Four of the best braves fought for my hand.
Spotted Horse would give a pure white

pony for his pale bride. I saw myself astride
that horse, my arms tight round a young man's
waist. His smooth thighs gripping
the horse near mine. But Dakota women
ride alone, and Spotted Horse already had
a wife. I searched for one sharp-featured face,
but Lightning Blanket was not among the four.

Days later, the fight between the men came
to blows. Lightning Blanket broke it up.
His lovely mouth curled; he spit. I still remember
his words. *Fools. It shames me to see warriors
fight over a worthless white woman.*
More, but I lost the will to understand.
The four fell silent, then began again,
squabbling like dogs over a bit of gristle
or bone. I turned away. That night,
the old ones helped me slip out,
and I began the long walk back
to my place in the world.

All so long ago, before my white husband
and I agreed to disagree, and I left, alone.
Before I found myself here, against
this strange western shore. Savages,
people called them. I might have stayed,
but for the sneer on one man's face.
Words wounded me surely as arrows.
So with words I had my revenge.
My heart grew dry and shriveled
as a wasted seed. When asked, I wrote
of their savagery, their cruelty,
of greasy brown faces and blank animal eyes.

Refused to recall kindnesses, how they fed me,
how they spared my life.
How the old ones loved me as their own.
I read of cavalry kills with greed, rejoicing
when Lightning Blanket was hanged.
Composing my story in flint and fire,
I basked in the hatred it inflamed.

Those days are gone, even the language
discarded with the memories bitter
as ash. Sometimes still, I see myself astride
a white pony, a warrior's bride. Impossible,
of course. Outside my window,
the sea fog moves like smoke,
spirits calling to me in a tongue
I refuse to understand.

The Strange Daughter

My child died of fever
that spring. How I mourned,
Cut my hair, my clothes, even
took the knife to my flesh, for she
followed my husband, killed
by white soldiers the winter before.
My loss a wound
that can't heal. And so

when the new fighting came
the soldier society promised me
a captive to replace the daughter
gone. That is our way.
But when they brought her
I was surprised. Not a child
at all, she was a grown girl, almost
as old as me. Still, I took her
home. Removed her former life
with her clothes. Made her one of us:
moccasins and a deerskin dress, my best
blanket. Braided her yellow hair.
Looks-at-the-Sky, I called her.

She was strange,
unbeautiful. Eyes like lake
water, skin pale as the underside
of a frog. Spoke in odd croaks
even the other captives couldn't
understand. But she was mine.
I fed her choice bits of meat.
Sang to her. Soothed her fears—

she was skittish as a deer.
Laughed with her. And when
the white men came finally and took
her away, her pale eyes filled—
a sky full of rain. Daughter.
I ran after her, keening.
My mourning began again.

In the Antelope Hills

During the last ten years of this quarter of a century, which she spent as a
captive among the Comanches, no tidings had been received of her. She had
long been given up as dead or irretrievable, lost to civilization. . . . There
was no longer any doubt as to her identity with the little girl lost and
mourned so long—but, O, so changed!

    —JAMES DESHIELDS, *Cynthia Ann Parker: The Story of her*
    Capture, 1886

In the season of the hoar frost—the earth
stiff as bone, in the season when the iced
grasses rattle in the clawing wind, then
they came. So cold that day. We women worked
butchering a buffalo. I showed Topsannah,
my little girl, how to warm her numb hands
in the rich red flesh. The meat
a blessing. Our hands gloved in blood.

We should have heard them coming,
heard the ring of iron hooves
on frozen ground. But we laughed
and sang as we worked, and they swept upon us
unheard, guns already aimed. White men,
their animal faces bristling with hair. I called
on the earth to open and shelter us,
but it would not heed my cries.
My sisters' blood congealed
on that indifferent soil.

I wished to die there too, with
my people. My eyes, those terrible
sky-colored curses, gave me away.

13

Taken prisoner, we passed through our camp:
all blood and ruin, even our ponies
slain. My husband's body face down
in the dirt, a lone dog lapping
at his wounds. My daughter and myself
captive. Only my son escaped.

They brought us here, to this shell
of a house, a tangle of rooms stiff
with silence and pain. What do they want,
these pale old people who call me
by a name I'd learned to forget? Cynthia Ann.
They saw in me the child lost years ago.
She is long dead. I am Naduah, wife
of Peta Nocona, mother of Topsannah
and Quanah. Comanche. I sang
my place in my family loud, sang
into their shuttered faces. And they
chattered back, peering into my eyes, imperious
as magpies. Topsannah, they clucked over
like hens, but here, I have seen
how the chickens—penned—turn against
the strange chick, beaks sharp as thorns.
Their eyes glitter with cruelty.

So slowly passed the months,
surely we were trapped in some evil
enchantment, and the same endless
days, rubbing one against another,
part of the spell. I prayed for release,
until my prayers wore thin
as the moccasins I fought to keep
on my feet. Release did not come

for me. But some cruel spirit
must have twisted my pleas, for Topsannah
sickened and died. In despair, I flung
myself through the window, but outside
the night—turned mocking and
unfamiliar—shocked me to stillness,
stopped my escape. The ache
in my bleeding body distant
as those whose loss I mourned.

They caught me, those strangers
who call me family. Brought me back,
tied me to the bed. Restrained,
like the hopeless animals they keep.
Each day they bring me food.
I will not eat, nor hear
their voices; I brush them away
like flies. Daily I am weaker,
my life grown faint with dreaming. There,
they wait, my husband and daughter,
and I talk to them, words rolling
on my tongue like bits of bright
corn. I need no other sustenance.
My body is white; my blue eyes
betrayed me. But my true people
await me. I will leave this body behind
and pass with them like rain
through the sweet grass and sage.

II

At the World's Fairs

In the Mammoth Temples of the Columbian Exposition

—Taken from a Catalogue of Exhibits, 1893

Ah, the White City!
    Dazzling displays from forty foreign countries! Exhibits
from all the states! The Realm of Rare Trees and Plants. A Ramble
among Fruit and Wines.
The Palace of Mechanical Arts.
    A chime of nine bells—they ring
    like the music of heaven, reverberating. Two century
    plants in bloom. Corinthian columns ablaze
    with imitation sunbeams. A silver statue of Columbus.
    The monster cheese weighs eleven tons. Medicinal mosses
    and enormous bamboos.
The Ferris wheel, the greatest piece of machinery on earth!
    Dog shows! Carrier pigeons! Bovine blue bloods!
    Blandishments of field and farm!

Then into the Department of Ethnology and the Midway Plaisance:
    Cairo Street and the Turkish Village mosques minarets camels
    donkeys dancing girls Nubians Eskimos dogs diminutive
    monkeys with lots of hair
And:
    TurksArabsSyriansSiouxArmeniansEgyptiansPenobscotsPersiansParsees
    PuebloIndiansSamoansLaplandersMalaysMexicansChinese all
    in native costume the livestock exhibit the torture dance
    a man who eats live scorpions and broken glass in front of savage
    huts the Soudanese perform wild dances and drone chants of
    love and war
sixty-nine citizens of Dahomey—in winter their bare feet bled;
Labrador Inuit who lived in twelve bark-covered huts—some died;

fourteen Kwakiutl Indians secured by Franz Boas;
    totem poles skin lodges a Winnebago
    mat house a guillotine trinkets
    and curiosities criminals' skulls brains
    of idiots anthropoids and those of the lower races

And finally, Our Uncle Sam's Place,
    the government building with its intelligent variety on display:
documents connected to the Dred Scott decision; the only
letter Jefferson Davis ever wrote to Abraham Lincoln; Sitting Bull's
cabin from the Standing Rock agency; the arms used in his arrest;
his buckskin shirt; dead
    letter curiosities: dolls axes tarantulas human skulls
    ostrich eggs molasses candy alligators thousands of things
    that never reached their destination war department novelties
    peculiarities
    of bird and beast hair of all sorts stuffed specimens of endangered
    species all imaginable sorts of leather petrified wonders
    from Arizona a pair of boots
    of human skin the back of an Indian chief's
    neck, neatly tanned well-cured skin
    from a young girl's breasts
    an extermination series

in the shrine of the white city:
    letters to Columbus from Isabella his commission appointing
    him Grand
Admiral of the Ocean Seas Vice-King and General Governor of all
the lands he should discover;
    the first cross erected in America a cannon
from the Santa María oh yes,
the fair was a harlequinade of the deepest and most lasting

significance, a highway of savage
and beautiful surprises all sanctioned
by the law of the land.

The Conjuror of the New Century

1893

Step right in, ladies and gents, step
right in and see the conjuror of the new
century, sample the wonders
he unveils. Years will wink past
with a snap of his fingers; his magic
lantern will reveal the glories
of the century ahead, splendor
spread before you like a vast
unsettled plain.

Enter into the darkened tent and there
he is, prophet of the new, the master
magician who makes years disappear. Terribly
tall, impossibly thin, his bony fingers scythe
across the table shrouded in midnight
cloth. What wonders he displays!
Years skitter past like hunted mice
and he flaunts miracles: cities ablaze
with infinite electric lights, ice boxes
that chill without ice, carriages without
horses, life without toil. His lantern
illuminates astounding scenes: a ship shooting
to the moon like an arrow, machines
that move through smoky skies, magic
boxes that store knowledge and spew
it out again. A miraculous machine age!
Opportunity for all, money to be minted, dreams
crafted in credit and cash. Coins appear
between his fingers like winking eyes,

multiplying for new kings of industry
whose riches assault the mind.

Now here's his lovely assistant, blindfolded,
scales in hand. Sprightly she steps
into his oblong box. Swords slide in; muffled
shrieks and her thin blood seeps out,
unnoticed. But don't look away! There's
always more! A mustard-colored jar
produces magic gases, and an entire
generation chokes and falls. This new
centurion is skilled in sleight
of hand, making people disappear:
six million vanish into air, ash. Entire cities
vaporized in twin exploding clouds.
He pulls trinkets out of an empty
hat: famine, war, and plague. A pyramid
of oranges transforms into a pile
of human skulls, all that remain
from the charnel of Bosnia and Biafra,
Cambodia and Kosovo, countries
whose names don't yet appear on the maps
unfurled in boardrooms and war rooms.
And there's still more. He hawks elixirs
to the citizens of this new world: pretty
potions consumed through needles
and pipes in Bangkok and Boston, from
Amsterdam to L.A. The takers fall down
like passenger pigeons blasted
from the sky, and the razor wire
of justice encircles those who remain.

What a century! Money and gunpowder
perfume the age! Riches unimaginable
for some, while others beg, cowering
on their corner of cardboard or concrete
in the wealthiest cities of this world.
Wonder and opportunities unfolding
like a paper fan. Then crushed. The conjuror
introduces his entourage: generals and CEOs,
presidents and peasants armed
with their tools of war—planes, money,
power, pistols. All followed
by vultures and flesh-eating flies.

From the audience, a frightened voice
pipes up: Terrible illusion, take it
away! Too late, he cries, too late.
The entry fee is already paid;
this future is yours. Welcome
to your new world, a century
of dishonor, suffering, and pain.

Photo of Inuit Woman and Child at the
Midwinter Exposition, 1894

Her eyes are sad as autumn come early,
autumn in the treeless arctic,
where no bright leaves balance
the coming chill. In her arms, her baby
just four days old and infinitely
precious. She is sad, but baffled too.
Who are these white-skinned strangers
with their voices of sea birds fighting,
these strangers who pay to peer
at her pain, who reach for her child.

She knows the dangers. Three months
she has dwelt in this village constructed
for the curious. Visitors pay at the gate
for the privilege of strolling through
the "genuine Eskimo village," enter
into her makeshift cabin where she sits
on a wooden platform strewn
with straw. Only the nights are her own,
when the crowds depart and her people
relax beneath unfamiliar stars.
The sound of her own language—pebbles
rolling underwater—soothes her.
A month past, another woman gave birth,
but the child, cursed by the strange,
soft air, turned fretful and died.

Even now, as the photographer
disappears beneath his cloth
like a hangman's hood, she remembers

her child's birth, how she squatted
in the straw on this unyielding
floor, her teeth clamped together
to contain her cries. The blood
from her bit tongue sharp
as the salt of the arctic sea. Outside,
the voice of a bored white man,
though she could not understand
his words: "these savage women
give birth without pain, easy
as a mare dropping a foal."
The smoke from his cigar wafted
through the window, gagging her.
The child entered into this world.

Now the white women come
to smile and coo, pay handsomely
for the chance to examine
mother and child, so unlike them.
They paw at the infant as they would
a pup. And she holds
her baby close: my son,
she thinks, will live.

That was long ago. The fair
has been dismantled, even those
who remember faded away
like the sight of streamers
snapping on the Midway, or the shouts
and sighs of the roller-coaster
riders. Even the Eskimo Village,
torn down, forgotten. Only
the photograph remains.

But once there was a woman
and her child—two lone
human beings captured
in the crowd's devouring gaze.

Cannibals

—At the World's Columbian Exposition, Chicago, 1893

Only twenty-eight years since the great
conflagration, since civil war, when
America gorged herself on her own
entrails. Only twenty-eight years,
and the reek of blood and ruin still lingered
in spite of the scent of money, fresh-minted
and cool. So they built a dream city
on the lake, a city all white
and new. Inside, collections
of things, of people, to show off
the continent Columbus claimed
to discover. And there, on the Midway,
billed as cannibals, 68 citizens
of West Africa: whole families,
mothers, fathers, children, and—wonder
of wonders—the warrior women
of Dahomey, who danced in a flash of swords.
They dwelt in a village they built
themselves—laughed, gossiped, butchered
an ox, which they offered to observers
as if those paying strangers were honored
guests at a village feast.

All this long gone, surviving only
in forgotten fair catalogues on dusty
library shelves. But I find an image
of a man: cheekbones wide,
lips sliding upward almost into a smile.
How handsome he is—close-cut hair

and dark skin, bearing regal as a king's.
According to the caption:
a Dahomey cannibal. In a collarless
tunic, he sits barefoot upon the grass,
around his waist, an American flag.

In a later picture, I see the same man,
flag a little more tattered, jacket now
missing buttons, his stance more
serious, one hand on a hip, no hint
of a smile. His somber stare asks
who is civilized, who savage?
He came from Dahomey, to see
the marvels of this world, and now
months later, he has felt the press
of crowds, seen tobacco spittle dribble
down his daughter's bare legs—sickening
symbol of a fairgoer's disdain. He has heard
the laughter, harsh as a carrion-eater's
cries, faced the insults hurled
like weapons by red-faced men
whose ladies titter and smile.

And he knows that his own people
endure in this land: his own people stolen
and swallowed alive, vomited up
on these shores; knows they somehow
survived the years of chains and auction
blocks, the slavery and sorrow and
rage. He knows all this. He stands
before the camera, a man wrapped
in a torn, striped flag. And he can see
into the future: humiliations heaped up

as on overfilled plates, long years
of struggle and still no end. He sees
the white hoods and crosses, the swastikas
and death rows, and the politer prejudice
that smiles as it steals souls. All this
he sees: a country that casually
consumes its own.

He traveled to this place freely,
in steerage, but not in chains. Earned
a small percentage of the take. Saw electric
lights and barbarism firsthand, heard
the anguished sighs of ghosts
who flutter over the blood-saturated soil.
His visions are written across his face,
but the caption only notes
that he and the others liked to drink
Chicago beer, and "when pinching winds
and frost attacked their bare limbs,
the Dahomians lost interest in everything
except return." October in Chicago,
and bare feet bled on the ice-fanged ground.

How you must have suffered—
the flag no protection against America's
chill. Was the journey worth
the pain? A hundred years later,
what I want to know is this:
noble visitors from Dahomey,
what stories did you carry back home,
when you returned, finally,
to civilization's shores?

Geronimo at the World's Fair

—St. Louis, 1904

By then he was old, conquered, or so
they said. Living on his reputation:
shaman, soldier, hostile Indian
made docile by the years
as prisoner at Fort Sill.
So they put him on display:
for two bits, people could watch him
pace like a chained wolf and hoot
their disdain. It didn't work.
He never forgot who he was,
born Goyahkla, the man who heard
his name called four times
in a trance, who had been touched
by power like a shaft of silver
sunlight. Renamed Geronimo,
power nested in his hands.
He called to the night and she
came to him, a black wool blanket
cloaking his people's escape.
He chanted down cures for the sick.
He could see the future, could hear
what was happening fifteen miles away.

At the fair, he sat most days
in a straight-backed chair, fashioning
bows and arrows to sell as souvenirs.
Clad in a rusty suit and a pair of moccasins,
he signed autographs for a dime, posed
for photos for two bucks. "The old man's

high priced," a visitor said,
"but he's the only Geronimo."

On days off, his worn moccasins
trod the sawdust paths of the great fair,
old hawk eyes dazzled by displays
of electric lights. Trailed by his guards,
the prisoner of war peeped
into Midway shows, even rode
the Ferris wheel, little magic houses
that rose into the sky like stars.
He marveled at a magician's skill:
the woman in the box, the sword's
descent, and the woman stepping out,
miraculously whole. All symbols
of the white man's power.

But they were only tricks, Geronimo,
not power, only sleight of hand,
like the tricks that brought you
to your knees, conquered.
Only you rose up, triumphing
to the end. Everywhere your name
was known; almost a hero,
you even rode in a president's
inaugural parade. Collecting the coins
they offered, you sold your likeness
but never yourself. They thought
they had you trapped, an old man,
a tamed toothless beast like the white
bear you watched fetch balls
on the Midway. They were wrong.
As the camera focused, you stared

straight back, thoughts clear:
I know who I am. Do you?
Even as they took the photo
into their hands, you were already
gone, laughter rising like a coyote's call
from a canyon half a world away.

III

SURRENDER

Surrender

He was the one I couldn't resist
his voice alluring as distant thunder
on a summer afternoon, thrilling me
with the possibility of danger and the promise
of rain. Like thunder, his voice offered
a thrill of pleasure; my legs went wavery
as water at his words. I left a husband for him,
a child. All I had were his stories,
the shimmery future he wove for me
as we lay in a sweat-soaked motel bed.
I believed it all, and so did he,
though that future was never quite
in sight. Now his words buzz like blue
bottle flies, nuisances I wish I could just slap
away. His hope faded with opportunities
that never arose, with the slow loss
of his looks—sandy hair turned dry and sparse
as the grass growing beside our trailer.
He still drinks his whiskey without water,
but in the morning his hands shimmy
like his old truck as he guides his doctored coffee
to his mouth. The bad boy collapsed
into this ruined man. Some afternoons, drunk
on memories and dollar shots, he flirts
with the girls bored enough
to find their way to this end-of-the-road
dive. He tries to spin his magic, and his voice—
it's still good—sugar smoky and smooth.
A couple of quarters in the juke box
and he asks them to dance, and sometimes
they do. He's no longer the agile

man who spun me into a trance,
now he lumbers along as the girls
gaze past him—outdated and pitiful
as a lame dancing bear.

Friends pity as they watch his pathetic
flirtations—with me sitting there at the bar,
sipping on my single beer gone warm.
And so many days, I pity myself, old now, stuck
in this dust-driven town, our trailer house
a fragile prison on the prairie, a battered tin cup
I can't seem to crawl out from underneath.
My life is not what I wanted at 18
or even 30, when I slammed the door
on one life and took this lesser one
instead. My first husband was quiet,
steady as a gentle horse. Dull.
But him, he was exciting as a summer storm,
as illicit sex, full of promises fire-engine red.
I slid into the front seat of his idling
truck, and he kissed me breathless, hand sliding
automatically between my thighs. And I
surrendered, swooned, like I never had
as a young girl. Pledged myself to him.

Surrender.
I thought I knew the meaning
of it then. Thought it was the way
I sunk onto the shoals of his life
like a skimmed stone. Now I see
it is something else, something
we both learned to do. It is all the suitcases
I didn't pack, all the bars I trailed him to,

the long, dead hours I worked
to support us both. It is the jobs he no longer
applies for, the way he slides instead
into the whiskey's amber depths, the way night
after night he sighs before slipping
into a comatose sleep without dreams.
And it is the way I stand by and watch,
the way I measure out my days
counting shot glasses and cigarettes—
the creeping paces of his approaching
death. Yes, I'm the captive
audience who doesn't flinch
from the failed trick,
from the long, slow plummet
to the netless ground.

She Pictures Herself with Him

She sees herself waking to the flood
of morning. Light engulfs the room.
Sees herself lift the sleeping
infant to her face, nose pressed
to the milk-sweet flesh, sucking
at its scent. Or sees herself in the garden,
sweat and soil staining her skin
summer dark. She thinks
this is how it could be. Sees herself
writing in the room with the view
of the sea. Sees herself kiss
the husband as he comes through
the door. Sees herself lean into him,
listening to his inventory of hours:
of meetings and arguments, of petty
hatreds—his voice sharp and unending
as a bale of barbed wire fencing.
Sees how her mind spins down,
clicks off and the dream goes gray.

See her strength, how she swims
every day, how she feels she could go on
forever, body breaking past
the limit of the lanes. And see
the town as imagined: tiny, picturesque,
a fine, friendly place. See it
as it is: insular, isolated, a fist
clenched against the wilderness,
a futile gesture.
See how she paces the town
as she does the pool. Yes,

see how the mountains reign
over her, magnificent and cold
as the fangs of snakes. See how she swallows
her fear with each breath. How she looks
to the sea as if to swim her way
free. How even the child is strange
to her. See how her eyes slide over
the walls of the lovely house,
how the new clothes are heaped
in a wreck on the floor. See
how she adds up her accounts,
the cost of this scene. And the mountains
hem her in like jaws shutting.
And the price of this picture
is her life.

Reunion at the Girls' Boarding School

I cross the room and there you are,
transformed: scotch on the rocks in one
manicured hand, perfect hair, perfect
makeup, and fine new lines
netting your eyes. And me,
I'm just the same, in an Indian
cotton dress and work boots, still out of step
among the high-heel pumps and pearls,
my face brown and bare. You see me coming
and whoop. Arm thrown 'round my neck.
Best friends. Yeah, we were best
girlfriends. Just the sight of you
brings it all back, the nights we'd worm
out of a window and pace the cobbled streets
past the elegant faces of those aloof
mansions, choosing the house we'd live in
one day. We'd walk for hours,
arm in arm, pausing before lighted windows
to dream. We thought life was like that,
all froth and fancy, a banquet
of pretty pastries we'd gorge ourselves on.
Our fantasies insubstantial as air
whipped into cream. But pleasing. We'd shiver
home near morning in the rain. Or weekends
at your place when we'd go wild: furious
riot of booze, of boys—anonymous shapes
we slammed our young bodies hard
against, too eager for any pleasure. Girl,
we were wayward and wild, always
doing exactly as we pleased. Now we grip
each other's hands and laugh.

Later, fresh scotch in hand, you relate
your tales: private college and a year
in France, debate team and crew. Investment
banker husband, inattentive but rich,
and the inevitable BMW. And me?
I've been all around the world—
state schools and youth hostels, in love
and out, wrote bad checks and poetry,
drove sled dogs and beat-up trucks.
And am I happy, you want to know?
I am. You light another cigarette
and your fine hands shake.
I married for money, you say, and shrug.
Silence. And I remember the afternoons
we laid on your bed, feet propped
against the wall, hammering out futures
for each other, bright as beaten
silver bowls. How you sat up once,
serious, grabbed my hand. *Let's never
turn out like the rest. Promise me,* you said.
All along, you envied them; I never knew. You
were a middle-class girl on her way up, and I
was too dark too poor too stubborn too much
the scholarship girl and too ungrateful to boot.
You spied the lure and nibbled; the hook
slipped in. Me, I was all bad mouth bravado,
the trash fish of the river never
cast to at all. The next year, I sunk back,
happy, to the public schools and you—firmly
hooked—were reeled away. And now
you envy me. Listen, poverty
is no purer than anything else.
I'm still the same, I please myself. And you,

you tell me that you walk the streets again
at night, measuring your lovely neighborhood
like a cage. The houses lit up, showy
as sparklers on a birthday cake, and again
you pause outside and watch, but now
you see the steel jaws ready to snap
shut on these exclusive traps. Too late.
You say you'd do anything to escape, even
chew your own flesh free. Anything
but leave. And so you creep
the shadowed streets like a cat,
that domestic beast deluded
into thinking herself wild. Your eyes glitter,
teary, as they catch the light,
and you're chasing a prey so elusive
you don't even know its name.

In the Season of Suicides

she slides her finger
across the barrel of a gun again.
She finds it beautiful: its snout
gray blue and pleasing,
the mechanism's smooth mesh
and movement as she draws
the chamber back. Now the barrel
rests in her mouth, the taste familiar
as her own blood. It is March,
but the earth is still rigid
with winter, the sky blue,
but cold as a marble slab.

It is the season of suicides.
Last month her neighbor
exploded like a star, ignition
sparked by a single shotgun shell.
He was twenty-two. And though
they'd never spoken, she recalls
his long reddish hair, how he'd wave
as she drove past, one hand held high
above his head. She never knew
his name. And her sister, too,
the body in the bathtub, the brown
plastic bottle submerged in the liquid
chill. But her they brought back.

Night drops like a curtain
on a stage. She mixes another drink,
settles in her chair. At her feet,
the dead neighbor's dog sighs

45

in its sleep. She thinks of herself,
images flashing past
like still photos on a screen.
She used to be strong.
Split her own wood. Lived
alone. She pictures herself
in her shooting class, legs planted,
blonde braid hanging straight down
her back as she raised her arms
to aim. She was a good shot.
At the range, the middle-aged men
used to eye her and smile.

Another picture clicks
into place. Her sister.
My sister is weak, she thinks.
Vodka and sleeping pills,
or the razor's red dance
along her wrists. Never quite
enough. Three attempts in two years,
didn't stop the husband
from filing the divorce.

There is no reason, really.
Yes, a man left her too,
but that was months past.
Still pain squats on her
chest like an incubus,
its breath sour, numbing and gray.
All winter she has existed,
slumped in this chair, and listened
to the fire's voice, to the darkness
settling heavily around the house.

The pistol comforting
on her thigh.

And now the nights
are shorter. Now summer beckons
like a young man waving.
But she is tired of it all: the cabin
she built herself, her sister's needy calls
at 3 A.M., the way shadow
gives way to light. She snaps the clip
into the gun, and the dog
jerks awake. Watches. In her mind,
a brilliant red peony
bursts into bloom.

Lost Country

I don't remember the moment
I stopped being a child. Memories
like a baby's blocks scattered
by a clumsy hand—which is the one?
The moment I saw my father's truck
in the driveway and I went still—hands
twisting to fists in my pockets?
Early autumn, and I was just coming back
from school. I was always home first,
so this could only be bad news:
someone hurt, dead, or him fired
or drunk. Maybe that wasn't it.
Maybe it was the instant I entered the empty
house—no sound except the slow
ticking of the kitchen clock and the bump
of a wasp at a window, wings grazing glass.
I called for my father. No response. Silence
settled like dust. Or was it the instant
I saw the attic door, ajar, and I stepped
forward, taste of fear flooding
my mouth like blood? Fear
of my father—his fists and his rage.
Maybe it was the moment
I was dragged into in dreams
for years. My father. One foot bare.
Shotgun cradled between his knees.
The blood on the walls still wet.

Maybe it was later yet, standing by his casket,
my brothers clutching my mother's
hands. Words unsaid, but heard

all the same: we depend on you.
I left school that year, not quite seventeen,
went to work at the foundry,
just like my old man. Maybe it was that first
morning, his battered lunch pail waiting
for me, our last name inked along the top.
Manhood a life sentence I was shoved into.
His buddies shepherded me through shifts
and after, through hours whiled away
with six-packs and shots. Just like him
I learned to drink my pain to sleep,
watched my brothers grow wary,
their ease ending when I entered the room.

Maybe the moment
I'm looking for is the one
I never saw except in dreams:
My father taking the stairs slow,
shotgun and shells in his hands.
He slumps into the kitchen chair
he brought up from below. Loads
the gun. Unties his shoe. Then he blows
my whole life to hell: my childhood
a distant country, and me
a trapped wasp buzzing
in an empty room.

Helen in Captivity

(for my mother)

Where are they, *les petites?* What have you done with your
children? Oh yes, I still remember, his words echo in my head, my
head a maze of rooms opening into locked empty chambers and
unexpectedly his voice, angry red and loud. What did he care about
the children? For him I did it. And who are you, peering into my
shuttered spaces, asking questions?

Open a door and there he is. Jean. Glacier blue eyes and that mobile
mouth, the slight sexy limp. I met him in a bar; he was gambling in a
back room. Understand how it was. War just ended, my husband
away in the steam and stink of the Pacific. And me still young and
pretty—yes, I was, once. I saw him when I could. Left the girls with a
neighbor, or alone. So what. Pat was eight then, old enough to look
after Sandra, the baby. At night when they slept, I slipped out to his
waiting car. Come with me; we'll see Paris, he said. His words
alluring as a sugar Easter egg—those fairy shells enclosing fanciful
candy landscapes. Inside the hollow egg was freedom, the boulevards
of Paris, a sugar city I longed to slowly suck the flavor from. But the
girls. Ah. *Les enfants.* Leave them with your mother.

This room is full of neon words, of names and emotions glaring
electrically in the air. *Whore. Unnatural. Go home and be a good mother.
Adulterer. You'll burn in hell.* The things my mother said to me. The
words flash like flares. The things she shouted. The things he said,
later, when he found out. *Where are they?* Other words, too. *Mommy.*
Tears. *Don't leave me.* Words jumble in the air, shrieking strobe lights.
Shut the door.

I never saw Paris. He took me to Montreal, that great frozen city on the river. Left me in that room above the bar while he gambled. He had never seen Paris himself, was a Quebec farm boy, freed from the war by his bad leg. Our nights were still sweet, but my dreams haunted: the child's fingers burning my skin like a brand. Her eyes, pale blue as a rain-washed sky. And the oldest girl, her stare direct, accusing. Hating. Their gazes whittling away at my flesh. I grew thin, wraith ridden. Too often alone in that room with my condemning dreams. And he began to lose interest. His eyes swiveling after a French barmaid, the real thing. She had seen Paris. He wanted to send me home, to my children, he said. And I was reeling drunk on a bottle of sweet red wine. Gone, I said. The girls long gone. And then his questions. Where are they, les petites? What did you do with them? The room echoing with his shouts. What did he care? Drowned them like kittens, I said and laughed. He slapped me hard. An orphanage, I said. For you. His face curdling like a glass of sour milk. He spat on the floor, his words flashing like swords I impaled myself on.

Shhhh. Open this door softly. Sandra is sleeping. Look how sweetly she rests, her hair veiling her face. My little angel. If she recalls that day she doesn't show it, when I loaded them on the bus to Milwaukee, held their hands as the door to the orphanage swung open. Left them with the matron. Pat, the oldest, was already hardened to life, her mouth set and sullen. Her eyes cursing me. She didn't even cry when I began to walk away. But Sandra, ah, the baby, only three, she clung to my legs and cried, a tiny human chain. Yes, I cried too, I suppose. But my eyes were on Paris, the boulevards and champagne, Jean's arm snug around my waist as we strolled. I pushed the child away. *I don't want you.* I did not. The door shut; I was free. In their sleep the children shift and moan.

Left alone in that gray city, snow swirling down, covering things better left behind. In that single room, where the neon flash of the bar below lit up the room like a ghost. In one room, but room upon room opened up in my head. A tangle of empty rooms, sharp corners angling into doorways, doorways that opened into identical empty chambers. So alone. Even my nightmares fled. And when I took his razor to my wrists, it was only an attempt to find my way out, to leave a trail of red that would lead me out of those cold narrow halls.

Yes, I have seen Paris. She is a gray city, a whore straddling a frozen river, a river that hides the evidence of what she has done. Of children drown for a man, drown and lost forever, though their voices still cry out from beneath the ice. A city of cold monuments of snow and dirty clouds. She smells of spilled champagne and cigarettes and blood spilled long ago in forgotten rooms. Old whore, hated even by her bastard children. Oh, you say I never left Montreal, that I have no visitors. It isn't true. See, he comes, Jean, leading my little girls, so lively in their summer clothes, their hair floating around them like the robes of drowned angels. We talk of Paris, where we go every spring. My lover and my daughters. Their voices echo: shouts, recriminations, childish voices whispering my name.

Sometimes it is so hard to find them.

Sometimes I wander these long twisting halls, room opening onto empty room, a city of echoing spaces.

Some of the rooms are haunted.

The Century Plant

Leaves like swords and thorned. Agave. Century plant. You showed me how to see beauty in its sheer stubborn survival. Leathery gray and alien—weird fantasies sprouting in the desert's meager soil. The desert you loved, your home. You told me about pulque, the liquor distilled from these plants. Taught me Spanish words I loved to roll on my tongue. *Querida. Mi corazón.* You were rare and precious as water. Intoxicating. *Agua dulce, agua santa.* Desert rain.

My first lover, my only one. We fell into one another like happy children, full of play. And when the laughter stopped and we looked into one another's eyes, I felt I'd found something lost long ago, something I never knew I couldn't live without. Your lips my spring of strength. Your hands on me firm and sweet. My hands on you. Love a flash flood. Beneath your mouth I bloomed. We spent three months entwined like canary vine. Your arms a refuge where I forgot to be afraid. But when I went home at semester's end, dinner at my house was like a summer storm gathering. Inconsequential conversation as the pressure built. I hinted. A relationship, I said, someone I liked, no pronouns used. On the TV, that omnipresent hum in our house, a gay pride parade and me watching covertly with a guilty gaze. I know some gay people, I said, my voice tentative and shy. My father thundered, and the channel roughly changed. My mother smiled sweetly—God loves the sinner but hates the sin and doesn't it just turn your stomach? My own stomach achurn. I bowed my head, and the storm of my parents' censure passed over me. I counted the days till I could return to you.

But graduation loomed like the frown on my father's face. *You don't have to go back,* you told me. You imagined a life for us in a little trailer in the desert. We'd get jobs waitressing, and each night we'd come home to the other's waiting arms, to talk, to laugh, to return to our bed, the wellspring of the miracle between us. I tried to imagine it—the trailer cradling us, your tongue licking me alive every night like a mother bear with her cub, but beyond the tinfoil walls a thorny darkness condemned and the night was too alive with stings: scorpions, centipedes. *What are you afraid of?* you asked me. I was afraid of everything: afraid of being shoved from the rickety raft of my family's love, afraid of the way I felt when I touched you, the way my heart resurrected, a dry plant in the rain.

Back at my parents' house, fragile as a refugee whose country is in ashes, I followed my family to church, was offered friendship, salvation. I surrendered with the chaste ecstasy of those who learn to deny desire. My days cluttered with Bible lessons and passionate prayer. They taught humility and submission and sin—the words bitter bread I swallowed as if starving, my hunger proof of my need. Still I dreamed of you. I prayed more, my prayers clouding the air like smoke, rising up to God's flinty face. In time, I married. My husband thought me a virgin, and so I was—innocent of men.

There is a fire on earth that burns much hotter and sweeter than hell. I've felt it. Eternity is now, a lingering death I face every day. Extinction a relief. Relief from the dry empty vistas of my days, from the fire my flesh falls into dreams. From memory, that hair shirt I put on every day. From desire that shackles me still to a past I must never admit. Year by year, I begin to understand. I chose my own punishment. I am the sinner doomed to an exemplary life. I am the century plant that bloomed once and failed. I long for what must never come again—the flood in the desert, flower and flame.

The Tattoo Artist

I go to get a tattoo. A butterfly, coy flutter on an ankle. I take a little something to relax. I fear the needle, that gleaming serpent's fang. But then I think of the tattoo artist's arms, the way an amethyst panther prowls up one forearm, the way along the curve of his bicep a dolphin dips into a fantastic sea of starfish and seaweed, the way bright phantasms brood beneath his shirt. I call to say I'm coming. His apartment hums with heat. He smiles seriously as he lets me in; he's naked except for a pair of shorts. And the tattoos. His body blooms with color: a tropical garden teeming with orchids and brilliant birds of paradise. A vine—riotous with scarlet flowers— snakes up one leg, glides beneath his shorts, slinks up the beach of his belly. His back fecund with fantastic beasts, a bridge between dreams and waking. A mermaid weeps indigo tears that transform into fans of diminutive fish. A Chinese dragon exhales a shower of stars. A herd of plum-colored horses, hooves sparking saffron light. Hallucinatory color, the electric glow of pigment injected beneath his skin. A palimpsest of symbols, illustrations from a trance. I would read those images like braille, my fingers, tongue traveling along the labyrinths of ink, discovering entire continents between his shoulder blades, along a thigh. I tell him what I want. He frowns, his face the only part of him unmarked, a blank banner floating above the tumultuous images parading across his chest. Then he shrugs. "A butterfly, if you like. But it is so ordinary, so unlike you. Maybe something more . . . original?" I nod. He smiles and his teeth catch the light like pearls. A tangerine tiger shivers, tensed to leap from beneath bamboo shadows. A leaf green snake undulates on his chest. "Where?" My ankle seems an unworthy offering, too tame, too far away from those undiscovered continents of desire. I pull my T-shirt over my head, proffer one breast. And he busies himself with paper and pencil, and he rubs the pattern onto my skin. And he slips his hand under my breast, holds it reverently, as if weighing gold. My nipple hardens at his touch. Then the needle whines to life, begins its burn on my skin and I can barely hold still—it's like an itch you can't scratch—and the needle moves in and in and in and my bright blood eases out around it and I sink into the sea swirling and swelling on his arm. "Do you like it?" he asks, hand still cupping my breast, dabbing at the beads of blood and sweat with a cloth moist as a mouth. And I rise through his waves to see. I open my eyes and images surface like leaping fish. On my left breast, a violet flower blooms. Into its trembling depths a hummingbird—all emerald green and garnet—inserts its narrow beak, sucking the nectar from the flower's long throat. The wings vibrate with the rise and fall of my gasped breath. The flower stems from a bottle green vine that fades into my skin. If I could only pluck that vine, follow it like a thread into the maze of patterns yet to be traced. I can almost see them, the ghostly phosphorous of tattoos waiting to be needled in, waiting for the hand of the dream master, the vision giver, the tattoo artist. "Oh, yes," I say. "Oh, yes." My flesh demands design.

The Bad Wife

The bad wife doesn't cook gourmet meals.
The bad wife doesn't flatter your boss.
The bad wife isn't a good housekeeper,
        doesn't wear frilly aprons
        or take pies to the neighbors.
The bad wife doesn't ask about your day.
She doesn't balance the checkbook,
        do laundry, or fill up
        the car with gas.
She doesn't drive safely.
The bad wife doesn't say she loves you.

The bad wife wears a black leather
        miniskirt, red spike-heeled boots
        and a blonde wig.
She doesn't wear panties.
The bad wife flirts with strangers in bars
        you didn't know existed. She drinks
        bourbon straight, smokes home-rolled
        cigarettes and lets the smoke shoot
        out her nose.
The bad wife carries a .38 in her purse
        and knows how to use it.
The bad wife fights back.
        She is not afraid of anyone.
        Not even you.
The bad wife gets her nipples pierced,
        gets a tattoo that says Mike.
        Which is not your name.
The bad wife takes your credit card, charges
        two pairs of silk, paisley-print boxers,

a bottle of scotch, some Kama Sutra oil.
A hotel room. You get the bill.
The bad wife doesn't come home at night.

The bad wife is a scream of pleasure
        heard through the wall of a motel room.
She glows in the dark.
She is blue neon at night.
The bad wife is a roller-coaster ride
        you never want to end
        though you're sick and shaking
        with the pleasure.
She's slow poison and you don't want
        the antidote.
She's ruthless.

The bad wife opens up your chest
        with one long-nailed finger.
She takes your heart in her teeth and shakes it
        like a terrier with a rat.
She's already swallowed your soul.
        And spit it out—insignificant
        stone.
The bad wife grins, terrier-toothed, and
        you let her back in—to your house
        to your heart to your bed.
The bad wife will never leave you.

The Good Wife

I'm deranged by desire. It's a cyclone that sucked me up, swept me away. Ten years married, happy, then it hits—a gale-force wind, and I'm torn from my moorings. I'm the worst kind of fool, struck by the arbitrary god of unacknowledged lust—that freak accident, the one car crash on a dry road at noon. I'm a witch who conjures up the spirit of my desire. I orbit him like a moon. And him, he's ordinary as air. I'm oxygen starved. He's the north star I navigate by. He's a tropical island; I want to shipwreck on his shore. My star sapphire. My freshwater pearl. He's the chain gang I'm shackled to; he's razor wire, searchlights, and the baying of the hounds. A heat-seeking missile. He's my terrorist insurrection, my Holy Resurrection, my only indiscretion. He's the smoky slow-burn of *chipotle* on the tongue. My golden idol. My gospel revival. He's hashish sweet and languorous—my body's one desire.

But I love my husband. I love my husband, and I've never strayed. I don't intend to start. Yet for the moment, I ride along on an avalanche of my own making. I'm crazed. I scan the sky for signs, portents, which way will it go, will I get him or not—all options impossible. I'm trapped in the torture chamber of love. I see him and I turn frantic, an acquisitive squirrel, storing bits of him away, images to subsist on between sightings: slim fingers splayed around a coffee cup, eyes a confusion of green and gray, the tendrils of hair curling damply on his temple. Oh what big eyes I have the better to see him with anew! His mouth mobile and fine as he talks—who cares what he says—I don't hear his words, only watch that mouth, those lips a well I long to drink from, and I think just one kiss, which leads to others, just one button unbuttoned or maybe two, just unbutton his shirt, run my hands through the fine hair on his chest. Just once. Let's just make love once. Oh, once is never enough. I gaze at his face as he talks and I think, you know, I really want to fuck you. And he stops talking, keen glance at me. Did I say it? No, but he smiles as he talks—does he know? I'm struck dumb, a pillar of salt, punished for my unruly desire. My skin flushes, eager for his touch.

At night I dream in my husband's arms, his body familiar and dear. And I think I'd give it all up, my life, the husband I love, my reputation, for one honeyed afternoon in a hotel room with this man. When I see him again, our hands brush—accident or purpose? Innocence or caution, I can't decide. His proximity makes me tremble; I scare myself. Only his inaction saves me. So when he speaks, smiles, says my name, I carefully compose my reply. And I wait for love's flood tide to subside.

Tsunami

As if I have no eyes. But I'm no blind fish, navigating sunless
waters sightlessly, transparent as innocence and as dumb. I see. I see
how her gaze swivels toward him, sunflower following her sun. Face
bright and stupid with joy. How she once was with me. Tell-tale
tremble in her voice, I remember that, too. She makes love to me as
if I'm transformed, an undiscovered territory she's crazy to explore.
But her eyes are closed, lips parted, and I don't want to hear the name
that rests there like a breath she can't expel. And him, he can't match
his gaze to the moment, can't find the appropriate response. He looks
at me when he speaks to her, as if her glance would turn him stone-
silent, still his too eloquent tongue. Or he looks too long when she's
turned away, his face gone soft and avid as an infant's, guileless,
greedy. Dinner like dozens before, but now he praises the food as if it
was as precious as the pearls of her nipples, pearls he longs to roll
beneath his tongue. Or maybe has. Who knows. Both of them start
when they hear the other's name: that deer-in-the-headlights stare. I
want to run them both down, or blast on the horn to break the spell.
My friend, my wife. I hate them both—their cotton-candy infatuation,
stupid spun-sugar dreams. The sudden silences between them
pummel me like a summer storm of hail. He avoids my eyes, never
says her name. She walks about the house, distracted, self-satisfied as
a cat or a woman well loved. The wondering eats at me like acid.
Does he run his hands across the soft swell of her hip? Does he know
the breathy sigh she releases in love, like she's just now settling, softly,
back to earth? Is it love or lust, and which one should I fear more?
Years, they never noticed one another, and now they're two mice
hypnotized by the serpent's stare, edging ever closer to the thing that
will swallow them up. If they're not lovers yet, they're close to it,
dancing after sex, that pied piper. And I'll be left standing alone,
outside the rock wall snapped shut. Nothing will ever be the same. I
can already hear the rending silence they'll create. I want to scream

into their narcotized faces: If you two touch, you'll bring down drought and pestilence, famine, war, and plague. The sun will go supernova; the earth will shift on its axis; mountains will rumble; lava slide into the sea. At night, I dream a tidal wave towers over our town like a cobra before its prey. She swoons, oblivious, in her lover's arms, and I watch the wave approach, helpless before its force. I wake before it hits, but I know how the dream goes, how we wait for disaster, the water's rage and crash. Our lungs swell with seawater as we drown.

Psalm

My husband wakes me at dawn
and gazes upon me with eyes the muddy green of the great rivers
that wend their way through civilizations so ancient
we've forgotten their births, their names;
My husband has hands that touch me
like the passionate flutter of a dragonfly's wings;
My husband's arms are wide and warm as a tropical lagoon
I collapse into, cradled by waves;
My husband's beard is a tangled jungle of orchid vines
    and hibiscus,
and I lose myself in his vortexes of vivid green;
My husband's mouth is sweet as the berries plucked on a barren
    slope,
berries fermented to a liquor rivaling the work
of a thousand industrious bees, a liquor much rarer;
My husband's body is an altar of marble, smooth as water,
an altar laden with offerings: rich pelts of rare animals,
blossoms of plants that flower once every thousand years, musky
    perfumes;
My husband has the teeth of a god—
they shine like mountain ranges ringing hidden kingdoms—
they nibble at me like fish bearing mouthfuls of pearls;
My husband has ten-thousand-mile legs—they stride across
    continents,
simmer like steam through my jungles, move like night across my
    tundra,
yet he is always by my side;
My husband smells of bread and new wine, of the spiced smoke
of sandalwood burnt in the hide tents of desert tribes;
My husband's voice seduces the dead, causes them to leave their dusty
shadowed paths for the clatter and heat of the living;

63

his voice turns whole seas red, makes tigers shed their stripes
  and dwell
like vivid feline suns in bamboo hills;

He is graceful as a birch, as a young girl, *like princess Diana,*

I am *like*

as a bow newly stretched from green wood;

He laughs like leaping antelope; *like Mother Teresa,*

he dwells in my mansions forever;

he annointeth my skin with his own.

My cup runneth over.

IV

The New World

The Alchemist's Assistant

Lovely as the native birds that fly overhead unseen,
the alchemist's assistant feeds him corn gruel
and chilies, sweeps the pitiful grate. Sings
in her primitive way. Gathers
the base stones, silent as severed tongues,
which the alchemist cannot force into gold.
In the windowless tower, the workshop is frigid
with his frustration, dumb with his dogged
desire. He has grown old here and still
the stones refuse to yield. He mutters incantations
and spells, pale eyes unfocused, while around him
the world is littered with substances precious
and rare: the assistant's skin—copper ore, her black
pearl eyes, and outside the lapis sky and cinnamon
hills. The myrrh-thick garden between her thighs.
He caresses the stones as another man
would her breasts. In his dreams, she rides him
like a nightmare, a vortex his secrets
are sucked into. Her hands roam over
his parchment skin and she plucks
at his power like a string. And laughs.
She treats him like an arrogant child—
with his foreign formulas, his old world
computations, his numerical desires.
He's stubborn and inert as stone.

Tucked away in his tower
of useless words, he withers.
But the alchemist's assistant leaves
the workshop every day. She gathers the stones
by calling their names—clicks of her tongue,

syllables of silver, turquoise, and jade.
They flock to her and sing
their stories. For her, the stones unlock
their shy mysteries and shine. For her,
mistress of the new world.

The Witch's Lament

There are all sorts of magic: things I do
with burning herbs and chanted
words, or the spells I weave
into my hair—wreathes of rosemary
and mint to lure a lover. There is the magic
of my hands and thighs, the only tricks
I needed to draw you to my bed.
There is the magic we wove together,
whispering words and swimming
into one another's skins. And when
I rode you, time after spent time, that was no
witch's trick, only the old enchantment
between man and woman, the way we fed
our bodies' foolish cravings.

I let you see my secrets. You watched me wring
the neck of a grouse, let me feed you
its heart simmered with saffron, onions,
and thyme. A simple spell. The bones
I ground to powder and put away
in the cobalt jars that line my shelves. Blue
bottles of mysteries you'd rather not plumb.
You've seen my book of shadows, know
that with bladder wrack and broom
I could call the storms, raise
the wind, call the waves that break the ships
and drown the unlucky, the incautious,
the unloved. But I do not.

As autumn wanes to winter
the storms seethe, the ones

that rend men and their toy
boats, then spit out bodies
of the drowned—decorous with kelp.
The wind around my walls waxes rich
with voices, the darkness beneath the trees
dense. As the light fades,
the path between me and your home
grows fainter; finally you fear
you will lose your way. Still you come,
but when you rise, sated, from my bed,
you pluck up and pocket the loose curls
of your hair. For now the roots I work
seem ominous, my eyes clouded
with soothsaying and second sight.

In the end, you fear what draws you, fear
what you've released—the fierce hawk
of your own desire. The storm inside you
could level this place. And so you retreat,
call me a witch. A story old as your kind—
I've seen it before, and didn't need any
second sight. You fear what you can't control
or possess, and snap your heart shut
like a miser's money box. I know
you won't be back. I sigh, brush away
ash from the spent incense.
It's just like you: cold and insubstantial,
though once it burned so sweet.

In Your Absence

I drink too much and cheaply—
a jug of mountain burgundy,
Pabst Blue Ribbon bought by
the case. I skip meals and smoke
clove cigarettes. In your absence
I recall the delicate bones
in your wrists, the way your hair
curled up in swirls on your neck,
the way your hands felt
on my breasts. In your absence
I make love to myself
with your hands. I close my eyes
and recreate your face, freshening
my memory with the picture
by the bed. I wear your old T-shirt
to sleep. In your absence
I read the letters you send—tissue
thin paper and foreign stamps. You tally
the sights you've seen: a night market
and the Mekong, river taxis
and Buddhist temples, a strip show
in Pattpong. You're off to Singapore,
Saigon, and Katmandu. No date
mentioned for your return.
I look for the words the letters
lack, and the things we haven't said
seem enormous—acres of   white space
I collapse into between words. You tell me
the women are beautiful as butterflies
there, the days sultry and mango sweet.
You leave no forwarding address.

If I could reply,
I'd tell you this:
last night, missing you so much
I thought I would disappear, I leaned back
against the sauna wall, watched
a man's head rise from between
these grieving thighs. In your absence,
I pulled him to me and kissed
his wet mouth, drew him deep
inside me. "You're so beautiful,"
he said, and even in your absence
I was, skin sueded with sweat,
golden in the candle's light.
You should have seen me.
I thought of you then, almost
called your name. That's how it was
all night: names and faces blurred,
identities sloughed away
like memory, until you were him
and he was you and the only name
I knew for sure was my own—
that brown, bitter seed.

This is how it's been
in your absence.

Young Wife Dreaming

Sleepy in the sun, she's splayed out
on the bed of his truck, a caught
catfish frying flat in the pan. His fingers—
ringed with engine grease—
weave into hers and he says
let's get married.
The words shock her awake.
We'll head south, start our own life.
She thinks of her family home, bleak
as a campfire gone cold. *Yes. Yes.*
She's just turned 18. She'll climb
into the passenger seat, let
this clever-fingered boy
drive her away.

But the Sunshine State's not all
it appears, and they are never quite
alone: there's his sweet-smiling sister
with the snapping turtle soul,
who rummages through drawers till she finds
the girl's hidden journal, which she reads aloud
as she laughs; there's his crepe-faced mother,
who runs one long-nailed finger across
the top of the fridge and says *when's*
the last time you cleaned here; who throws
away the catalogs collected from the community
college and says *there's no need*
for that now—have a baby, settle down;
and there's her own sweet lover turned
strange, grown greedy in the pleasure
of possessing, so he grills her about the grocery

store: *what took you so long, who*
did you see? until even her thoughts
are not her own: *what are you*
thinking, tell me!

And it is the year of the ERA, which founders
like her own dreams now crushed
to a scarlet pulp like the tomatoes she packs
at the canning plant. All day on the line
in the heat and clatter she thinks she is beaten
as that red fruit; though her husband's hands
are gentle, his love forces her through a sieve,
cans her, puts her down on a dusty shelf
in a failing country store while somewhere else—
somewhere else!—life passes, a shiny
silver dollar, aching to be spent.

She only wants simple things: unstained
clothes, classrooms, conversation, people
talking of more than baseball and babies,
washing powder and pistons. She dreams
of stepping out of this life as neatly
as a child skips out of a circle
that's been chalked on the sidewalk. At night
her young husband clings, mutters
her name. As if he knew.

For already, just one year in,
the thought glides into her mind, a shy
guest who slips into a chair, awaiting
notice. Divorce. She rolls
the word over in her mouth, taste

74

familiar as RC cola, cool liquid
on her parched tongue,
dark brown and sweet.

Over the Chilkoot Trail

I still recall the details of that day,
how he trotted up the walk
calling out in a voice bell-clear
with excitement. How I stepped outside,
pie in my hands heavy as an infant.
"I'm going to the Klondike," he said
and the pie dropped, crust exploding,
yolk-yellow crescent moons of peaches
bleeding into the dust. My skirt
and shoes sticky with the spattered syrup.
And him, contrite, handling me gently
as a frightened animal. As he wiped
at my clothes, I felt myself go silent
as stone. Hours later, the ants drew
thick black lines through the ruined pie,
drunken insects drowning in golden juice.

When we stood there, before the long throat
of the Chilkoot trail, I thought of those ants again.
A dusting of snow like the sugar I sifted
on my pies, and broad lines of men surging
up the trail like disorderly ants. Among them
was my Joe—my dead mother's walnut
dining table strapped to his back. Sentimental,
yes, but I had foolishly insisted, so he struggled
up the pass, his love for me borne heavily
by his body. I waited with sacks
of provisions, foot resting on my Singer
sewing machine, another whim Joe patiently
carried. Single men laughed, called us
cheechakos, fools, worse. But I had seen

the young wives left at home, hands restless
with loneliness as they fiercely knitted items
they sent north. I would not remain behind.
Joe said it was only for a season, but I also knew
how men, like ants, grow drunk and drown
in their dreams of gold. When Joe shouldered
the last bag onto his back, I followed him up.
Reaching the top, mud spattered, winded, sore,
I gazed down on the town turned tiny,
and the sea beyond. Then I turned my back
forever on the known world.

The years flew by like the first snowflakes
of fall. Two years in Dawson City, where
I saw men grow rabid as dogs out of greed,
saw men shot over cards in the gambling house,
saw fresh-faced girls turn bitter and hard
in a season. We never found gold.
I sewed miner's clothes, an endless procession
of parkas and pants, and I served many a meal
at my mother's table for a dime. It kept us alive.
Two years in the Klondike, till the dream
of gold played out, and the boom faded
from the town the way color drains
from a dying rainbow trout. Then we moved on,
traveling down the Yukon's great spine.
A year spent in a canvas tent in Circle City,
where I held a baby on my lap as I sewed,
wedged between the walnut table and the barrel stove.
Then here, to this town on a gentler river,
to the house Joe built, where the table now resides.
We ate here together every day until he died.

Now I sit here, my hands caressing
every scratch and scar in this old wood,
telling you how half a century ago
your grandfather lugged a table
through the wilderness for love. My fingers
read the marks in the wood like braille,
a lifetime's tally of journeys, of people
and places long ago left behind.

The White Professor Holds Forth on Indians

Wind breathes the snow horizontal,
flakes like scraps of paper ripped
in fury from the pages of a book.
All semester he has droned on, voice
arrogant and incessant as the thrum
of the fluorescent lights. She watches the snow,
watches herself grow silent, diminished
by his onslaught of words. "Our culture,"
he says, hearkening back to Europe's clattering
shores. "Our culture," he says, meaning his,
as if he does not see the darker faces
on the fringes of the class, the studious
young black man taking notes, the Asian girl
toying with her field hockey stick,
and her. All unseen, as if these ivy-choked
structures could contain only one color.
His words are a river. She is battered
along from rapid to rock to deceptive
calm. He is not an evil man.
He is the Native American specialist.
What he doesn't understand makes her gasp.
He turns all she knows strange. Her own life
made exotic, a painted trinket turned out
for tourists. And the world he takes for granted
is foreign to her, a chambered nautilus of chilly
rooms lush with the rustle of certainty
and paper money. She has never been
so lost before.

And then a tiny miracle, tossed like coins
to a beggar's cup. He switches on a tape

and a woman's voice struggles through
the static of years. The song, in a language
unknown but familiar, rises like a flutter
of beautiful brown moths. Sitting there,
she can picture the singer, long dead
but resurrected: brown face finely
wrinkled as an autumn leaf, twin
gray braids, the familiar Indian body—
short, sturdy, thick-waisted. She thinks
of her own grandmother: smell of wood smoke
and home-tanned moose hide, fry bread
and Labrador tea. Her brown hands
grip the desk in longing. And she swims
into the song like a salmon fighting
its way upstream—a muscled sleeve
of silver scales slipping through the net.

White Lies

On learning that Allakariallak, who played Nanook in his film Nanook of the North, *died of starvation less than two years later, filmmaker Robert Flaherty wrote in his diary: "Nanook was dead. Poor old Nanook!"*

Nanook he christened you, creating
a false fixed-image of the arctic:
seal hunt turned slapstick comedy,
an ice-windowed igloo, and you,
the fur-clad clown at center stage. All lies,
fed to generation after generation, until more
white people than there were stones
on that northern shore knew your face.

You did what you were told. He'd pay
with credit at the store, and you agreed,
calculating the cost of a new rifle,
some good steel traps. 1921, and you took
what you could from the white strangers
who wandered north. So you donned
the parka he'd had made, carried the crude, useless
spears. Even pretended his local lover was your wife.
Rolled into blankets of skins, you joked
with her as the camera rolled, laughing
at the strangeness of the white man's whims.
Sometimes you played tricks, left him alone
on the tundra and moments later
he'd be lost and helpless as a child.

But he played tricks too, abandoning
the arctic for points south, never claiming
the child his lover bore. His trade credits trickled

so quickly away—some sugar, a bag of flour—never enough
for the rifle or traps. He even took back
the spears, the fur parka. All that remained
was the film you never saw, and what it grew to be—
a great mythical beast with Flaherty fastened
to its flanks like a fattening fly.
Foolish Nanook lives forever, while you
starved to death two years later in the last storm
of a killing spring. Flaherty would say
that the film of your life faded
to blizzard white, the great hunter
vanquished, dying alone. He'd be wrong.
He thought he had you fixed—fine specimen
of a vanishing race, but your spirit was too great
to be contained. Nanook was only an ill-fitting
mask you wore awhile, then tossed away.

That final spring, as you wait—weak
from hunger—for the storm to pass, you remember
meals you've eaten, the taste
of dried fish dipped in seal oil, bear's liver,
rich and raw, sweet berries, even the strange
taste of the black disk that spoke,
the gramophone record Flaherty made you bite
on the film. All gone. Now you fill your mouth
again with a handful of snow, gritty
and insubstantial as the movie he made.
You know you will die here, but you are not
alone. Ancestral spirits shimmer
in the blowing snow. Years from now
your black-eyed granddaughter
will chant to her child your name—one

among many—a link in the chain
of memory extending like the long reach
of winter days. Allakariallak. Allakariallak.
Itivimiut hunter. Your death comes
before the storm passes. And the white bear
of your last breath stalks out across the sea ice,
ascending to the snow-rich clouds.

Seal Woman Accepts the Sacrifice

I

Through water, your gaze tracked my
powerful kicks, smooth spirals, my gliding
dives that lasted ticking eternities.
Breaking the surface, my brown skin
bejeweled with light, my eyes
liquid, warm, your body stirred
in response to my gaze.

On land, I disappointed.
Thick-limbed, muscles cloaked
in a cocoon of fat. Too dark, too heavily
pelted, too strange. You wanted
a mermaid, that stupid slut your kind invented
to pose like a centerfold on rocks,
all fishy scales and vapid smiles. No such luck.
Only I exist, and I would never trade the sea
for a mortal man. I do not make sacrifices;
I demand them. You look away. Too late.
You are chosen, your weakness festering
within you like a rotting tooth.

II

When I look into your eyes I see
lines of men like you, retreating
back across the ocean in your rickety
ships. Generations of men, making fortunes
in timber, stones, fur, and oil. Things torn
bleeding from ocean, earth. I see
you clubbing my children, breaking their skulls—
candy crushed between your teeth.

You colonize my people, pollute
our holy places. You never learned
to take with respect, to leave something
behind. For your kind, who see only
in opposition, it is all or nothing,
and you never choose nothing.
Behind your eyes, I see your brain, buzzing
with abstractions, numbers scratched
into the flayed skins of trees, stick
images representing naught.

When you look in my eyes you see
no one but yourself, reflected back ten times
your size. The brutal conquistador,
the butchering yellow-haired soldier, the policeman
bloated with law. You do not see
me, my people, our mysteries:
images wrought in smoke
and spray. You cannot live
in my element, but I live in both.
Ocean surrounds me: above and below,
beside, inside, tidal currents thrumming
in my veins. I breathe air, but live here,
where the sun filters down
through the waves like rain, where the silence
echoes with the songs of whales.
Here things change form as easily
as patterns drawn in sand.
But you do not see. To you, my eyes
are flat button-black,
meaningless and dumb.

III

I seek you out.
I'm the dark-skinned whore
you pay to fuck, the women
whose bleeding hands stain the cotton
they pluck from your fields, the mute
illegal maid who moaned gibberish
when you raped her on your bathroom's
tiled floor. The olive-skinned attorney
you meet at a hotel bar.

Like all those women,
she repulses and attracts, stubby body
firm beneath its sheath of fat.
Her hair a rich black pelt. Awkward
in her pin-striped suit, she stumps about
in ill-fitting heels. She invites you
for a swim, and you picture her clothes
falling away like flesh from the bone,
a jack-knife dive as she slices the water.
She would move as quickly as a fish,
as a storm at sea. Slick.

First dinner. Sushi.
She snaps it up in a frenzy, voracious.
Her appetite excites you, disturbs.
You talk of the business of your kind,
of forests cleared, of oil extracted. Progress.
She encourages you in her hoarse voice.
Come up while I change, she says.

She steps into the room naked
but for a seal-skin coat of storm

gray. She keeps it on as you force her
to the floor. She claws
your face, your back, marks you
with her teeth. Draws blood that beads
on the silver seal-skin coat.

IV

Even your ancestors knew
the visitor from the sea. Generations
later, arrogance piled upon bloody
arrogance, you have forgotten all
your kind ever knew.
Seal is only fur, or the silly beast
that balances a ball on its snout.
These hands will not clap for you,
and see, my flippers have claws.
My teeth snap bones like water.
I shift shapes, come out of the storm,
off the sea ice, out of a blinding wind.

You lack respect.
You fear the sea.
You should.

V

Relax in the ocean and it
will cradle you, rock you home.
You cannot. You desire only
to possess, destroy.
You mock my seal body.
You forget my teeth, my claws.
And yet I draw you.

In your strength and arrogance
I accept you. In your weakness
and ignorance, I accept you. In your hatred
and destruction, I accept you. As judgment
and redemption, I accept you.
With your life as sacrifice, I accept you.

Come swim with me, that you may drown.

And I will adorn your corpse
with coral and cables of kelp, and schools
of glittering fish will nibble at your flesh.
Rocked in the waves, you may become
beautiful and whole once again.

In an Angry Season

They've gone to witness the river's mad
descent into spring. The heave and thunder
as the ice shakes itself from the shore,
the way the frozen slabs—pachyderm gray
and similarly sized—shear one into
another as the Yukon shudders awake.
From a hawk's height the pipeline bridge
mocks the river's riot and churn. Perched
there, they watch—then his pale hand
turns her tawny face to his and
they kiss, roar of loosed ice echoing.
They are both just nineteen.

And now they sit, hands clutching brown
bottles, in a one-room cabin turned
tavern. A wooden counter, scabbed over
with men's names. A Naugahyde couch,
slouching by the door. One man at the bar,
face flat in a puddle of beer.
His phlegmy snores. The room choked
with smoke. The one they call Dirty Dave
is telling a story: "We picked up this squaw
hitching her way into town. Weren't no room   .
in the cab, so she crawled in back. I went after her.
I said, whatever you hear, boys,
don't stop this truck." Laughter. He grins,
gap-toothed and mean. Leers at the girl.
"I like it when they fight." She shivers.
Twists at a strand of her black hair.
Her boyfriend draws her closer.
Six men—they've been drinking

all winter. One girl. One nervous
boyfriend. A mining camp a hundred miles
or more from town. And Dave stares
at the girl. "What do you think of that?"

And she thinks: There is so much evil
in this world. And she thinks of her hand,
squeezing the bottle till it breaks, scraping
this man's face to bone with the shards.
And she thinks of the river, how in some
angry seasons it could not be contained—
bridges snapped like thread, whole villages
devoured by the Yukon's flood and fury.
And she hears the river shift and growl.

About the Author

Lisa D. Chávez is a Chicana mestiza writer, teacher, and traveler
who was born in Los Angeles on the winter solstice and raised in
Fairbanks, Alaska. She has an MFA from Arizona State University.
Her first book of poetry, *Destruction Bay,* was published by West End
Press in January 1999. She has had poems published in various maga-
zines and in the anthologies *¡Floricanto, Sí! A Collection of Latina Po-
etry, The Floating Borderlands: Twenty-five Years of U.S. Hispanic Lit-
erature,* and *American Poetry: The Next Generation.* She has also
published nonfiction and is currently at work on a memoir of growing
up in Alaska. She is an assistant professor at Albion College in Michi-
gan, where she lives with her husband and two dogs.